Contents

Scottish Food

Scotland's cuisine is very distinctive and is often based on traditional staples such as fish, mutton, beef, potatoes and oatmeal. Listed here are some traditional Scottish dishes and ingredients, so that the next time you visit Scotland, you'll be able to tell your bannocks from your rumbledethumps. Some of the dishes mentioned here are featured in this book, so get cooking!

ARBROATH SMOKIE A wood-smoked haddock still produced in small family smoke-houses in the east-coast fishing town of Arbroath.

BANNOCKS (OR OATCAKES) A barley and oat flour biscuit baked on a griddle. Nowadays, bannocks are often eaten with cheese or butter. There are several traditional recipes for home baking and many manufacturers still operate in Scotland.

BLACK BUN A very rich fruit cake made with raisins, currants, finely-chopped peel, chopped almonds and brown sugar with the addition of cinnamon and ginger. It takes its name from its very dark colour.

COLCANNON Known as Rumbledethumps in the Scottish borders, this is a dish found in the Western Islands of Scotland and also in Ireland. It is made from boiled cabbage, carrots, turnip and potatoes. This mixture is then drained and stewed for about 20 minutes in a pan with some butter, seasoned with salt and pepper and served hot.

CROWDIE A simple white cheese, made from the whey of slightly soured milk and seasoned with salt and black pepper. The seasoned whey is squeezed in a muslin bag to remove any excess water, put aside for two days, then rolled in oats and served.

FINNAN HADDIES In the late 19th century, as fast transportation by train became available, the Aberdeen fishing village of Findon (pronounced locally as "Finnan") began producing lightly smoked and delicately flavoured haddock (haddies) which were of a much finer texture than anything available up until then. They were an immediate success, and have been used in many different recipes ever since.

FORFAR BRIDIES These are said to have first been made by a travelling food seller called Maggie Bridie of Glamis in the county of Angus, previously known as Forfarshire, hence the name. Forfar Bridies are similar to Scotch Pies but, unlike these, the meat filling (usually beef) is crimped into the pastry case. The pastry may be either plain or flaky.

HAGGIS In his *Address to the Haggis*, Robert Burns said:

Fair fa' yer honest, sonsie face,
Great chieftain o' the pudden race!

Haggis is perhaps the best known Scottish delicacy, and made properly it is delicious. The uninitiated can be put off by the ingredients, however, as haggis is made from sheep's offal. The heart, lungs and liver of a sheep are boiled, then minced and mixed with beef suet, oatmeal, onions and some spices. This mixture is traditionally placed inside a sheep's stomach and sewn closed, although nowadays beef intestine, commonly used for sausages, is more often used. It is then cooked by further boiling for up to three hours, although the part-cooked haggis can be cooked in the oven, which reduces the risk of it bursting.

PORRIDGE A simple dish made of boiled oatmeal, porridge needs to be cooked slowly and stirred continuously to avoid lumps, traditionally with a spirtle – a wooden stick about 30 cm/12 inches long. Traditionally, crofters in the highlands of Scotland would make a large pot of porridge at the beginning of the week. Once cool, it would be cut into slices that the crofter would take for his lunch each day. These days, it is more commonly eaten as a hearty breakfast with the addition of milk and sugar.

SCOTCH BROTH A rich stock is traditionally made for this soup by boiling mutton, beef, marrow-bone or chicken. Any number of different vegetables can then be added, depending on personal preference. Carrots, garden peas, leeks, cabbage, turnips and a stick of celery can all be used.

SCOTCH PIES These popular, self-contained pastry pies are filled with minced meat and are the original fast food. The pies are made in special straight-sided moulds, roughly 7.5–8.5 cm/3–3½ inches in diameter and about 4 cm/1½ inches deep. A pastry lid covers the meat about 1 cm/½ inch below the rim, leaving a space at the top that can be filled, if wanted, with hot gravy, baked beans, mashed potatoes or whatever is preferred.

SCOTTISH BEEF The Aberdeen Angus breed of beef cattle are now reared across the world, reknowned for their rich and tasty meat, which makes excellent steaks. Good butchers will still hang and prepare the meat in the traditional manner, although this is becoming increasingly rare.

SCOTTISH SALMON The Rivers Tay and Tweed are major salmon fisheries. Since Victorian times, these and other rivers have hosted wealthy fishing parties on the estates of the aristocracy. Poaching (illegally catching) salmon is an equally traditional activity.

More recently, huge fish farms have been established in the sea lochs on the west coast of Scotland. These are major commercial sources of fish, although the quality is not considered to be as good as wild, river-caught salmon. Scottish salmon is used in hundreds of different recipes, but thinly sliced and smoked as a starter is one of the most popular ways of eating it.

STOVIED TATTIES (OR STOVIES) Stovies are a potato-based dish, designed to use up left-over meat and vegetables. To make them involves frying onions in beef dripping, adding scraps of meat and left-over vegetables along with cubed potatoes and water, and leaving this to cook. The resulting stovies have the consistency of chunky mashed potatoes.

Cheese & Onion Oat Pie

Ingredients
Serves 4

1 tbsp sunflower oil, plus 1 tsp
25 g/1 oz butter
2 medium onions, peeled and sliced
1 garlic clove, peeled and crushed
150 g/5 oz porridge oats
125 g/4 oz mature Cheddar cheese, grated
2 medium eggs, lightly beaten
2 tbsp freshly chopped parsley
salt and freshly ground black pepper
275 g/10 oz baking potato, peeled

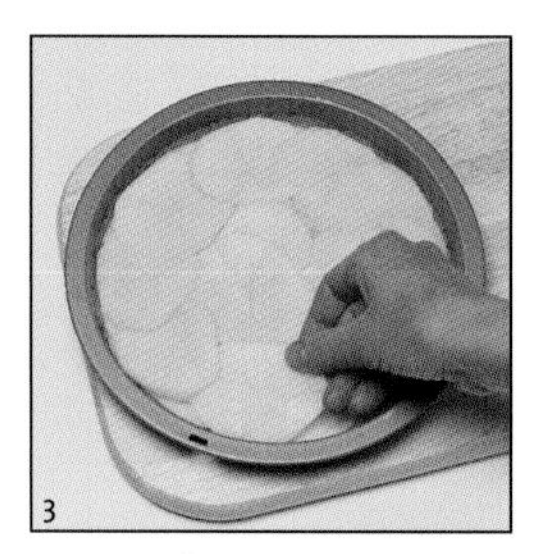
3

6

1 Preheat the oven to 180°C/350°F/Gas Mark 4. Heat the oil and half the butter in a saucepan until melted. Add the onions and garlic and gently cook for 10 minutes, or until soft. Remove from the heat and tip into a large bowl.

2 Spread the oats out on a baking sheet and toast in the hot oven for 12 minutes. Leave to cool, then add to the onions with the cheese, eggs and parsley. Season to taste with salt and pepper and mix well.

3 Line the base of a 20.5 cm/8 inch round sandwich tin with greaseproof paper and oil well. Thinly slice the potato and arrange the slices on the base, overlapping them slightly.

4 Spoon the cheese and oat mixture on top of the potato, spreading evenly with the back of a spoon. Cover with tinfoil and bake for 30 minutes.

5 Invert the pie onto a baking sheet so that the potatoes are on top. Carefully remove the tin and lining paper.

6 Preheat the grill to medium. Melt the remaining butter and carefully brush over the potato topping. Cook under the preheated grill for 5–6 minutes until the potatoes are lightly browned. Cut into wedges and serve.

Arbroath Toasties

Ingredients
Serves 4

175 g/6 oz
smoked haddock
175 ml/6 fl oz milk
2 tbsp plain flour
25 g/1 oz strong, hard, grated cheese
1 egg, separated into white and yolk
salt and freshly ground black pepper
4 slices of buttered toast

1 Heat the smoked haddock in 150 ml/¼ pint of the milk in a saucepan. Bring to the boil, reduce the heat, cover and cook for about five minutes or until the fish flakes easily with a fork. Remove the fish with a fish slice and flake.

2 Mix the flour with the rest of the milk and then stir into the milk in the saucepan. Bring to the boil and cook for two minutes, stirring continuously until thick.

3 Stir in the cheese, egg yolk and flaked fish. Season to taste with salt and freshly ground black pepper, then heat through.

4 Whisk the egg white until it is stiff and fold into the fish mixture with a metal spoon.

5 Put the toast on a grill rack and spoon the fish mixture on to each slice of toast.

6 Place under a hot grill until the topping is lightly browned and serve immediately.

CHEF'S TIP
Arbroath is a fishing town on the east coast of Scotland that is famous for its smoked haddock. If haddock is unavailable, however, smoked salmon can be used instead.

1

3

4

Scotch Pie

Ingredients
Makes 8–10 pies

For the meat filling:

450 g/1 lb lean lamb, minced
pinch of mace or nutmeg
salt and freshly ground black pepper
150 ml/¼ pint gravy

For the hot water pastry:

450 g/1 lb plain flour
pinch of salt
175 g/6 oz lard
7 fl oz/200 ml water, approximately
milk for glazing

You will also need:

glasses or jars, approximately 7.5–8.5 cm/3–3 ½ inches in diameter, to shape the pies

1 To make the meat filling, mix the minced lamb, spice and seasoning together in a bowl. Put this to one side while you make the pastry.

2 To make the pastry, sift the flour and salt into a warm bowl, making a well in the centre of the flour. Melt the lard in a small measure of water and, when it is bubbling, add to the flour and mix thoroughly.

3 Take a small amount of pastry (remember the mixture should make 8–10 pies, with their tops), and form into a ball. Keep the rest of the pastry warm while making each pastry case. Roll the pastry out and shape it around the base of a glass or jar approximately 7.5–8.5 cm/3–3 ½ inches in diameter. Make sure there are no cracks in the pastry. Trim round the top to make it even.

4 As the pastry cools, remove the glass and continue until you have about a quarter of the pastry left to make the lids. Fill the cases with the meat and add the gravy to keep the meat moist.

5 Roll the remaining pastry and use the glass or jar to cut the lids to size. Wet the edges of the lids, place over the meat and press down lightly over the filling. Pinch the edges and trim. Cut a small hole or vent in the centre of the lid to allow any steam to escape.

6 Glaze with milk and bake for about 45 minutes at 140°C/275°F/ Gas Mark 1. If the pies are not eaten immediately, they can be stored in the refrigerator. Always ensure that they are properly reheated before being eaten.

Swede, Turnip, Parsnip & Potato Soup

Ingredients

Serves 4

2 large onions, peeled
25 g/1 oz butter
2 medium carrots, peeled and roughly chopped
175 g/6 oz swede, peeled and roughly chopped
125 g/4 oz turnip, peeled and roughly chopped
125 g/4 oz parsnips, peeled and roughly chopped
175 g/6 oz potatoes, peeled
1 litre/1¾ pints vegetable stock
½ tsp freshly grated nutmeg
salt and freshly ground black pepper
4 tbsp vegetable oil, for frying
125 ml/4 fl oz double cream
warm crusty bread, to serve

1 Finely chop 1 onion. Melt the butter in a large saucepan and add the onion, carrots, swede, turnip, parsnip and potatoes. Cover and cook gently for about 10 minutes, without colouring. Stir occasionally during this time.

2 Add the stock and season to taste with the nutmeg, salt and pepper. Cover and bring to the boil, then reduce the heat and simmer gently for 15–20 minutes, or until the vegetables are tender. Remove from the heat and leave to cool for 30 minutes.

3 Heat the oil in a large, heavy-based frying pan. Add the onions and cook over a medium heat for about 2–3 minutes, stirring frequently, until golden brown. Remove the onions with a slotted spoon and drain well on absorbent kitchen paper. As they cool, they will turn crispy.

4 Pour the cooled soup into a food processor or blender and process to form a smooth purée. Return to the cleaned pan, adjust the seasoning, then stir in the cream. Gently reheat and top with the crispy onions. Serve immediately with chunks of bread.

CHEF'S TIP

For a lower-fat version of this soup use semi-skimmed milk instead of cream, when reheating.

1

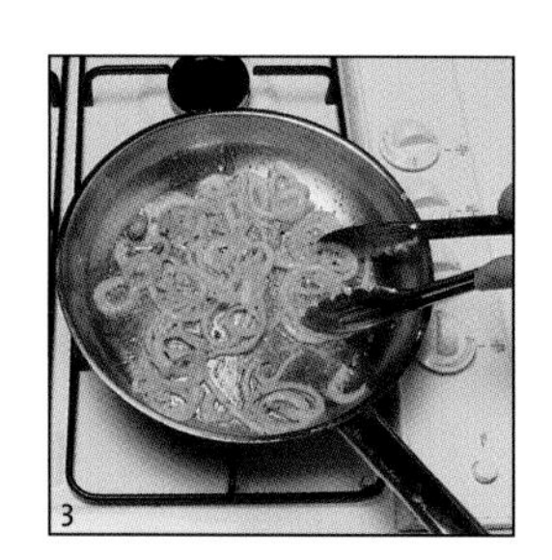

3

4

Cock-a-Leekie Soup

Ingredients

Serves 6

1 boiling fowl, about 1.8 kg/4 lb in weight, including legs and wings
3 rashers of streaky bacon, chopped
2.25 litres/4 pints of stock or water
450 g/1lb leeks, cleaned and cut into 1 inch pieces
bouquet garni of bay leaf, parsley and thyme
salt and freshly ground black pepper
25 g/1 oz long-grain rice
100 g/4 oz prunes, cooked and stoned (optional)
1 tsp brown sugar
freshly chopped parsley, to serve

1. Put the fowl and bacon in a large saucepan and cover with stock or water.
2. Bring to the boil and remove any scum from the surface.
3. Add three-quarters of the leeks (green as well as white sections), the herbs (tied together in a bundle), some salt and pepper and return to the boil.
4. Simmer gently for 2–3 hours, adding more water if necessary.
5. Remove the bird. This can either be used for another course, or you can cut the meat into small pieces and add them back to the soup – it should have some pieces of chicken in it when served.
6. Add the rice, the drained prunes, if using, and the remaining leeks and simmer for another 30 minutes.
7. Check for flavour – add the sugar if needed – and serve with a little chopped parsley.

CHEF'S TIP

Prunes are a traditional ingredient in this recipe, which dates from the 16th century. It is often served at Burns Suppers and St Andrew's Night dinners, though the prunes are sometimes omitted.

Cullen Skink

Ingredients
Serves 6

1 large smoked haddock, about 900 g/2 lb in weight
1 medium onion, finely chopped
1 bay leaf
salt and freshly ground black pepper
900ml/1½ pints milk
225 g/8 oz mashed potato
2 tbsp butter

To serve:

freshly chopped parsley
triangles of toast

1. Cover the smoked haddock with water in a shallow pan, skin-side down. Bring to the boil and simmer for 4–5 minutes, turning once.

2. Take the haddock from the pan and remove the skin and bones.

3. Break the fish up into flakes, return to the stock and add the chopped onion, bay leaf, salt and pepper. Simmer for another 15 minutes.

4. Strain the mixture, removing the bay leaf but retaining the stock and the fish. Add the milk to the fish stock and bring back to the boil.

5. Add enough mashed potato to create the consistency you prefer. Don't be afraid to make it rich and thick.

6. Add the fish, reheat and check for seasoning.

7. Just before serving, add the butter in small pieces so that it runs through the soup. Serve with chopped parsley on top, accompanied by triangles of toast.

CHEF'S TIP

Skink was originally made with a shin of beef, which can be substituted for the smoked haddock in this recipe. The name of this soup comes from the fishing village of Cullen, in Morayshire.

3

5

7

Cheese-crusted Potato Scones

Ingredients
Makes 6

200 g/7 oz self-raising flour
25 g/1 oz wholemeal flour
½ tsp salt
1½ tsp baking powder
25 g/1 oz butter, cubed
5 tbsp milk
175 g/6 oz cold mashed potato
freshly ground black pepper

To finish:

2 tbsp milk
40 g/1½ oz mature Cheddar cheese, finely grated
paprika pepper, to dust
sprig of basil, to garnish

1 Preheat the oven to 220°C/425°F/Gas Mark 7, 15 minutes before baking. Sift the flours, salt and baking powder into a large bowl. Rub in the butter until the mixture resembles fine breadcrumbs.

2 Stir 4 tablespoons of the milk into the mashed potato and season with black pepper.

3 Add the dry ingredients to the potato mixture, mixing together with a fork and adding the remaining 1 tablespoon of milk if needed.

4 Knead the dough on a lightly floured surface for a few seconds until smooth. Roll out to a 15 cm/6 inch round and transfer to an oiled baking sheet.

5 Mark the scone round into six wedges, cutting about halfway through with a small sharp knife. Brush with milk, then sprinkle with the cheese and a faint dusting of paprika.

6 Bake on the middle shelf of the preheated oven for 15 minutes, or until well-risen and golden brown.

7 Transfer to a wire rack and leave to cool for 5 minutes before breaking into wedges.

8 Serve warm or leave to cool completely. Once cool, store the scones in an airtight tin. Garnish with a sprig of basil and serve split and buttered.

Trout in Oatmeal

Ingredients
Serves 4

2 large trout, skinned
small quantity of milk
50 g/2 oz fine oatmeal
1 tbsp sunflower oil

For the parsley butter:

75 g/3 oz butter
3 tsps lemon juice
1 spring onion, finely chopped
¼ tsp cracked black peppercorns
1 tbsp fresh parsley, finely chopped

To serve:

freshly cooked vegetables

1. If not already skinned, remove the skin from the fish.

2. Cut each skinned fillet of trout into four equal size pieces. Brush each portion with milk and coat with the oatmeal.

3. Place the trout on a baking tray, cover with clingfilm and place in the refrigerator for 20 minutes.

4. Warm the butter slightly to soften it and mash with a fork. Add the lemon juice, peppercorns and chopped spring onions and mix well. Add the parsley and mix again.

5. Form the butter mixture into a log shape and cut into rounds. Chill in the fridge until needed.

6. Add the trout to some heated oil in a non-stick frying pan and cook each side for two minutes, or until the oatmeal has become golden. Serve with the parsley butter on top and accompanied by some freshly cooked vegetables.

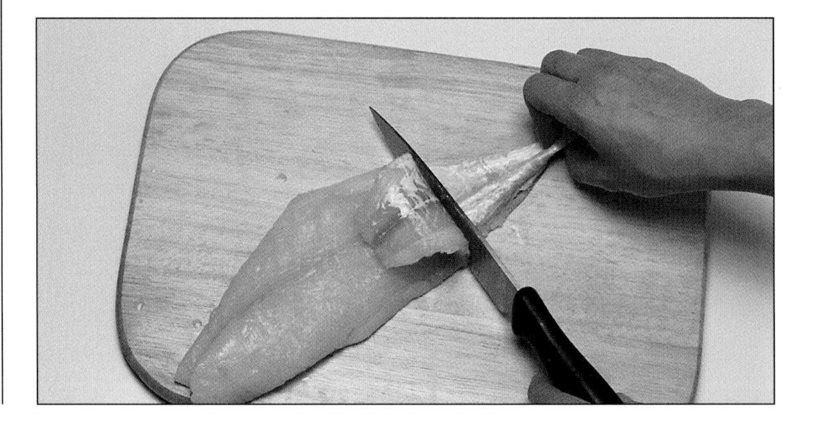

CHEF'S TIP

Rolling fish in oatmeal is a traditional Scottish cooking technique. You can do it with any fish, but trout, herring and salmon are particularly good when eaten in this way.

Potato Pancakes with Smoked Salmon

Ingredients
Serves 4

450 g/1 lb floury potatoes, peeled and quartered
salt and freshly ground black pepper
1 large egg
1 large egg yolk
25 g/1 oz butter
25 g/1 oz plain flour
150 ml/¼ pint double cream
2 tbsp freshly chopped parsley
5 tbsp crème fraîche
1 tbsp horseradish sauce
225 g/8 oz smoked salmon, sliced
salad leaves, to serve

To garnish:

lemon slices
snipped chives

CHEF'S TIP
Horseradish is a pungent root, usually finely grated and mixed with oil and vinegar or cream to make horseradish sauce. Commercially-made sauces vary in hotness, so it is best to add a little at a time to the crème fraîche and taste until you have the desired flavour.

1 Cook the potatoes in a sauce-pan of lightly salted boiling water for 15–20 minutes, or until tender. Drain thoroughly, then mash until free of lumps. Beat in the whole egg and egg yolk, together with the butter. Beat until smooth and creamy. Slowly beat in the flour and cream, then season to taste with salt and pepper. Stir in the chopped parsley.

2 Beat the crème fraîche and horseradish sauce together in a small bowl, cover with clingfilm and reserve.

3 Heat a lightly oiled, heavy-based frying pan over a medium-high heat. Place a few spoonfuls of the potato mixture in the hot pan and cook for 4–5 minutes, or until cooked and golden, turning halfway through cooking time. Remove from the pan, drain on absorbent kitchen paper and keep warm. Repeat with the remaining mixture.

4 Arrange the pancakes on individual serving plates. Place the smoked salmon on the pancakes and spoon over a little of the horseradish sauce. Serve with salad and the remaining horseradish sauce and garnish with lemon slices and chives.

1

2

3

Finnan Haddie Tart

Ingredients
Serves 6

For the shortcrust pastry:
150 g/5 oz plain flour
pinch of salt
25 g/1 oz lard or white vegetable fat, cut into small cubes
40 g/11/2 oz butter or hard margarine, cut into small cubes

For the filling:
225 g/8 oz smoked haddock, skinned and cubed
2 large eggs, beaten
300 ml/½ pint double cream
1 tsp Dijon mustard
freshly ground black pepper
125 g/4 oz Gruyère cheese, grated
1 tbsp freshly snipped chives

To serve:
lemon wedges
tomato wedges
fresh green salad leaves

1 Preheat the oven to 190°C/375°F/Gas Mark 5. Sift the flour and salt into a large bowl. Add the fats and mix lightly. Using your fingertips, rub into the flour until the mixture resembles breadcrumbs.

2 Sprinkle 1 tablespoon of cold water into the mixture and with a knife, start bringing the dough together. It may be necessary to use the hands for the final stage. If the dough does not form a ball instantly, add a little more water. Put the pastry in a polythene bag and chill for at least 30 minutes.

3 On a lightly floured surface, roll out the pastry and use to line a 18 cm/7 inch lightly oiled quiche or flan tin. Prick the base all over with a fork and bake blind in the preheated oven for 15 minutes.

4 Carefully remove the pastry from the oven and brush with a little of the beaten egg. Return to the oven for a further 5 minutes, then place the fish in the pastry case.

5 For the filling, beat together the eggs and cream. Add the mustard, black pepper and cheese and pour over the fish. Sprinkle with the chives and bake for 35–40 minutes or until the filling is golden brown and set in the centre. Serve hot or cold with the lemon and tomato wedges and salad leaves.

2

4

5

Traditional Fish Pie

Ingredients
Serves 4

450 g/1 lb cod or coley fillets, skinned
450 ml/¾ pint milk
1 small onion, peeled and quartered
salt and freshly ground black pepper
900 g/2 lb potatoes, peeled and cut into chunks
100 g/3½ oz butter
125 g/4 oz large prawns
2 large eggs, hard-boiled and quartered
198 g can sweetcorn, drained
2 tbsp freshly chopped parsley
3 tbsp plain flour
50 g/2 oz Cheddar cheese, grated

CHEF'S TIP
Any variety of white fish can be used in this dish, including haddock, hake, pollock and whiting. You could also use a smoked fish such as haddock or cod.

1 Preheat the oven to 200°C/400°F/Gas Mark 6, about 15 minutes before cooking. Place the fish in a shallow frying pan, pour over 300 ml/½ pint of the milk and add the onion. Season to taste with salt and pepper.

2 Bring to the boil and simmer for 8–10 minutes until the fish is cooked. Remove the fish with a slotted spoon and place in a 1.4 litre/2½ pint baking dish. Strain the cooking liquid and reserve.

3 Boil the potatoes until soft, then mash with 40 g/1½ oz of the butter and 2–3 tablespoons of the remaining milk. Reserve.

4 Arrange the prawns and sliced eggs on top of the fish, then scatter over the sweetcorn and sprinkle with the parsley.

5 Melt the remaining butter in a saucepan, stir in the flour and cook gently for 1 minute, stirring. Whisk in the reserved cooking liquid and remaining milk. Cook for 2 minutes, or until thickened, then pour over the fish mixture and cool slightly.

6 Spread the mashed potato over the top of the pie and sprinkle over the grated cheese. Bake in the preheated oven for 30 minutes until golden. Serve immediately.

1

4

6

Haggis

Ingredients
Serves about 4

set of sheep's heart, lungs and liver, cleaned by a butcher
one beef bung (intestine)
350 g/12 oz finely chopped suet
100 g/4 oz medium ground oatmeal
2 medium onions, finely chopped
120 ml/4 fl oz beef stock
1 tsp salt
½ tsp pepper
1 tsp nutmeg
½ tsp mace

1. Trim off any excess fat and sinew from the sheep's organs and, if present, discard the windpipe. Place in a large pan, cover with water and bring to the boil. Reduce the heat and simmer for an hour or possibly longer to ensure that they are all tender. Drain and cool.

2. Finely chop the meat and combine in a large bowl with the suet, oatmeal, finely chopped onions, beef stock, salt, pepper, nutmeg and mace. Make sure the ingredients are well mixed.

3. Stuff the meat mixture into the beef bung, which should be over half full. Then press out the air and tie the open ends tightly with string. Make sure that you leave room for the mixture to expand, or it may burst while cooking. If it looks as though it may do that, prick with a sharp needle to reduce the pressure.

4. Place in a pot and cover with water. Bring to the boil and immediately reduce the heat and simmer, covered, for three hours. Avoid boiling vigorously or you may burst the skin.

5. Serve hot with 'champit tatties and bashit neeps' (mashed potato and turnip or swede). For added flavour, you can add some nutmeg to the potatoes and allspice to the turnip or swede.

CHEF'S TIP
A traditional way of using up parts of an animal that might otherwise go to waste, properly made haggis is delicious. At Burns Suppers, the haggis is traditionally piped in and Burns' *Address to the Haggis* recited over it.

5

Forfar Bridies

Ingredients

Makes 6 bridies

700 g/1½ lbs boneless, lean rump steak or lean minced beef
50 g/2 oz suet or butter or margarine
1 onion, finely chopped
1 tsp dry mustard powder
50 ml/2 fl oz rich beef stock
salt and pepper,` to taste
700 g/1½ lbs ready-made flaky pastry

CHEF'S TIP

The original recipe for Forfar Bridies uses suet, but as this is not to everyone's taste, it can be substituted with butter or margerine.

1 If using rump steak, remove any fat or gristle from the meat and beat with a meat bat or rolling pin. Cut into 1 cm/½ inch pieces and place in a medium-sized bowl. Add the suet, or butter or margarine, together with the chopped onion, mustard powder, beef stock and salt and pepper and mix well.

2 Prepare the pastry and divide the pastry and meat mixture into six equal portions. Roll each pastry portion into a circle about 15 cm/6 inches in diameter and about 5 mm/¼ inch thick and place a portion of the mixture in the centre. Leave an edge of pastry showing all round.

3 Brush the outer edge of half the pastry circle with water and fold over. Crimp the edges together well. The crimped edges should be at the top of each bridie. Make a small slit in the top to let out any steam.

4 Brush a baking tray with oil and place the bridies on this, ensuring that they are not touching. Place in a pre-heated oven at 230°C/450°F/Gas Mark 8 for 15 minutes, then reduce the temperature to 180°C/350°F/Gas Mark 4 and cook for another 45–55 minutes. They should be golden brown – if they are getting too dark, cover with greaseproof paper. Serve immediately.

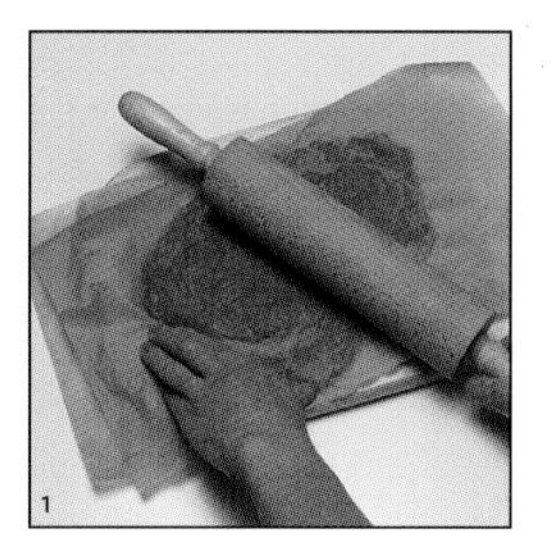

1

2

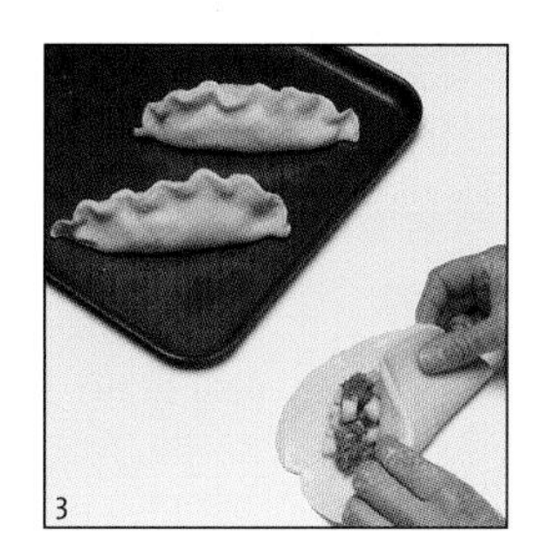

3

Shepherd's Pie

Ingredients
Serves 4

2 tbsp vegetable or olive oil
1 onion, peeled and finely chopped
1 carrot, peeled and finely chopped
1 celery stalk, trimmed and finely chopped
1 tbsp sprigs of fresh thyme
450 g/1 lb leftover roast lamb, finely chopped
150 ml/¼ pint red wine
150 ml/¼ pint lamb or vegetable stock or leftover gravy
2 tbsp tomato purée
salt and freshly ground black pepper
700 g/1½ lb potatoes, peeled and cut into chunks
25 g/1 oz butter
6 tbsp milk
1 tbsp freshly chopped parsley
fresh herbs, to garnish

1 Preheat the oven to 200°C/400°F/Gas Mark 6, about 15 minutes before cooking. Heat the oil in a large saucepan and add the onion, carrot and celery. Cook over a medium heat for 8–10 minutes until softened and starting to brown.

2 Add the thyme and cook briefly, then add the cooked lamb, wine, stock and tomato purée. Season to taste with salt and pepper and simmer gently for 25–30 minutes until reduced and thickened. Remove from the heat to cool slightly and season again.

3 Meanwhile, boil the potatoes in plenty of salted water for 12–15 minutes until tender. Drain and return to the saucepan over a low heat to dry out. Remove from the heat and add the butter, milk and parsley. Mash until creamy, adding a little more milk, if necessary. Adjust the seasoning.

4 Transfer the lamb mixture to a shallow, ovenproof dish. Spoon the mash over the filling and spread evenly to cover completely. Fork the surface, place on a baking sheet, then cook in the preheated oven for 25–30 minutes until the potato topping is browned and the filling is piping hot. Garnish and serve.

CHEF'S TIP

A traditional Shepherd's pie is always made from cold roast lamb, but you can make it with fresh minced lamb if preferred.

2

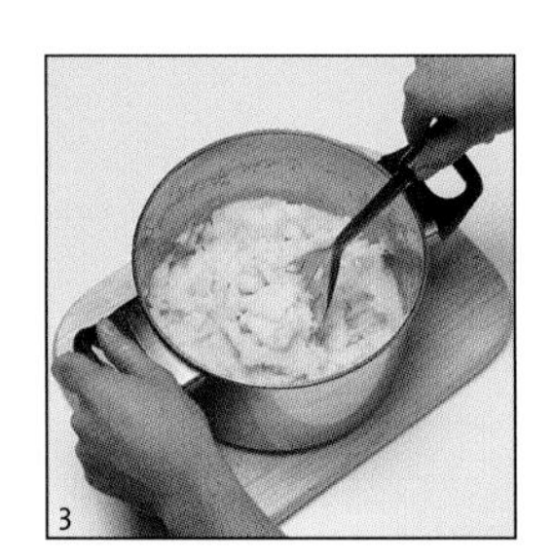
3

4

Chicken Bonnie Prince Charlie

Ingredients
Serves 4

4 chicken breasts, skinned and boned
a little flour, salt and freshly ground black pepper
1 oz butter for frying
2–3 tbsp of Drambuie
120 ml/4 fl oz chicken stock
4 apples
75 g/3 oz butter
250 ml/8 fl oz double cream
25 g/1 oz flaked almonds

1. Mix the flour with the salt and pepper in a large dish and use to flour and season the chicken breasts.

2. Fry the chicken breasts in hot butter on both sides. When they are well browned, sprinkle with Drambuie, add the chicken stock, then cover and simmer for ten minutes.

3. While the chicken is cooking, peel and core the apples. Cut them into thick slices and cook gently in butter until fairly soft – do not stir to avoid mashing.

4. Remove the chicken to a serving dish when ready and keep warm in the oven.

5. Make the sauce by adding more Drambuie, if required, to the stock left in the pan and gently stir in the cream. Heat but do not boil, then add the roasted flaked almonds.

6. Cover the chicken with the sauce and garnish with the sliced apple. Serve immediately.

CHEF'S TIP
Drambuie is a liqueur that combines fine Scotch whiskies with heather honey and other secret ingredients. The recipe is said to have been given to the MacKinnon clan by Bonnie Prince Charlie in gratitude for their help after the Battle of Culloden in 1746.

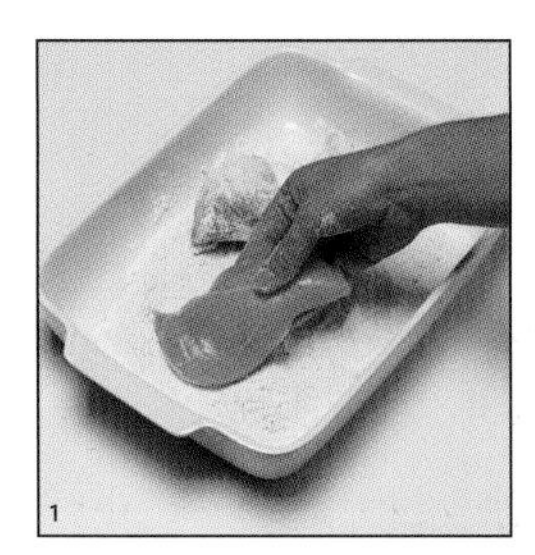
1

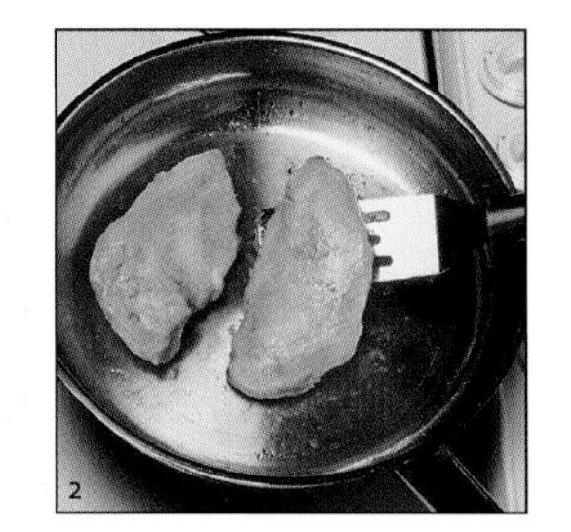
2

Roasted Grouse with Black Pudding

Ingredients
Serves 4

500 g/1 lb 2 oz new potatoes
4 sticks celery
1 leek
2 small courgettes
12 baby asparagus tips
8 baby onions
3 tbsp olive oil
50 g/2 oz butter
4 whole grouse, oven-ready
4 oz shallots
2 stalks of fresh thyme, chopped
25 ml/1 fl oz Madeira
300 ml/½ pint game or beef gravy
4 slices black pudding
salt and pepper to taste

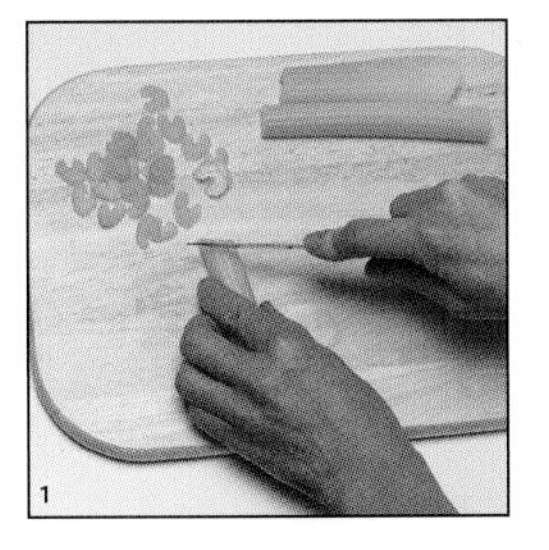
1

2

1 Place the new potatoes in a pan, cover with salted water and par-boil for 10–12 minutes. Drain and refresh under cold water until cool. While the potatoes are cooking, wash, trim and cut the celery, leek, and courgettes crossways in to 2 cm/¾ inch rounds at an angle. Leave the asparagus and onions whole. Lightly season the vegetables and brush with olive oil.

2 Preheat a griddle pan. Slice the new potatoes lengthways into quarters and fry them with the vegetables on the griddle to create a criss-cross effect. Remove and place on oven tray to reheat later.

3 Preheat the oven to 200°C/400°F/Gas Mark 6. Heat the remaining olive oil and 25 g/1 oz of the butter in a heavy-based frying pan. Season the grouse, place in the pan and seal on all sides. Place in a roasting tray and cook in the oven for about 20 minutes. Leave to rest for approximately 5 minutes.

4 To make the sauce, peel and finely shred the shallots. Melt the remaining butter in a saucepan, add the shallots and thyme and cover. Cook for about 2 minutes, until just transparent. Add the Madeira and the game or beef gravy and bring to the boil. Strain and set aside.

5 Grill the black pudding on both sides until cooked and crispy. Place on kitchen paper to drain for a few seconds. While the black pudding is cooking, place the vegetables back into the oven for 2–3 minutes to reheat. Place a grouse, a slice of black pudding and some vegetables on each plate, spoon the sauce over and serve.

Smoked Haddock Kedgeree

Ingredients

Serves 4

450 g/1 lb smoked haddock fillets
50 g/2 oz butter
1 onion, peeled and finely chopped
2 tsp mild curry powder
175 g/6 oz long-grain rice
450 ml/¾ pint fish or vegetable stock, heated
2 large eggs, hard-boiled and shelled
2 tbsp freshly chopped parsley
2 tbsp whipping cream (optional)
salt and freshly ground black pepper
pinch of cayenne pepper

CHEF'S TIP

If smoked haddock is unavailable, use smoked salmon instead.

1 Place the haddock in a shallow frying pan and cover with 300 ml/½ pint water. Simmer gently for 8–10 minutes, or until the fish is cooked. Drain, then remove all the skin and bones from the fish and flake into a dish. Keep warm.

2 Melt the butter in a saucepan and add the chopped onion and curry powder. Cook, stirring, for 3–4 minutes, or until the onion is soft, then stir in the rice. Cook for a further minute, stirring continuously, then stir in the hot stock.

3 Cover and simmer gently for 15 minutes, or until the rice has absorbed all the liquid. Cut the eggs into quarters or eighths and add half to the mixture along with half the parsley.

4 Carefully fold in the cooked fish to the mixture and add the cream, if using. Season to taste with salt and pepper. Heat the kedgeree through briefly until piping hot.

5 Transfer the mixture to a large dish and garnish with the remaining quartered eggs, parsley and a pinch of cayenne pepper. Serve immediately.

1

2

3

Crunchy Rhubarb Oat Crumble

Ingredients

Serves 6

125 g/4 oz plain flour
50 g/2 oz softened butter
50 g/2 oz rolled oats
50 g/2 oz demerara sugar
1 tbsp sesame seeds
½ tsp ground cinnamon
450 g/1 lb fresh rhubarb
50 g/2 oz caster sugar
custard or cream, to serve

1 Preheat the oven to 180°C/350°F/Gas Mark 4. Place the flour in a large bowl and cut the butter into cubes. Add to the flour and rub in with your fingertips until the mixture looks like fine breadcrumbs, or blend for a few seconds in a food processor.

2 Stir in the rolled oats, demerara sugar, sesame seeds and cinnamon. Mix well and reserve.

3 Prepare the rhubarb by removing the thick ends of the stalks and cut diagonally into 2.5 cm/1 inch chunks. Wash thoroughly and pat dry with a clean tea towel. Place the rhubarb in a 1.1 litre/2 pint pie dish.

4 Sprinkle the caster sugar over the rhubarb and top with the reserved crumble mixture. Level the top of the crumble so that all the fruit is well covered and press down firmly. If liked, sprinkle the top with a little extra caster sugar.

5 Place on a baking sheet and bake in the preheated oven for 40–50 minutes, or until the fruit is soft and the topping is golden brown. Sprinkle the pudding with some more caster sugar and serve hot with custard or cream.

2

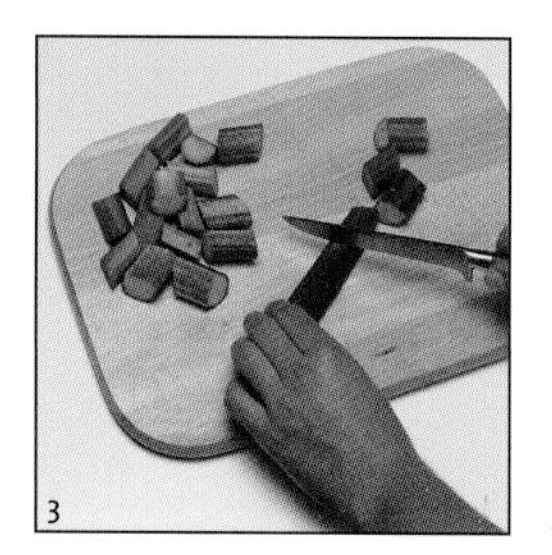

3

4

Scotch Pancakes

Ingredients
Serves 4

225 g/8 oz plain flour
pinch of salt
1 tsp cream of tartar
1 tsp bicarbonate of soda
5 tsp of caster sugar
1 medium egg
150 ml/¼ pint of milk.

1 Heat a griddle or heavy-based frying pan and lightly grease it.

2 Sift together the flour, salt, cream of tartar and bicarbonate of soda and mix in the caster sugar.

3 Create a well in the centre and add the egg and some of the milk. Slowly mix the flour into the egg and milk, adding more milk as you go until you have a mixture with the consistency of thick batter.

4 Drop a small amount of batter on to the greased griddle or pan – if it is the right temperature, bubbles should rise to the top in a few seconds. Drop in enough mixture to make several individual small pancakes.

5 When the underside is brown and bubbles are bursting on the top, turn the pancakes over and cook the other side. You may need to re-grease the pan after each batch.

6 Serve warm with butter and honey or jam. They are also delicious buttered and sprinkled with light brown sugar.

2

3

3

Dundee Cake

Ingredients

Cuts into 10 slices

175 g/6 oz butter
or margarine
150 g/5 oz caster or
granulated sugar
4 eggs
225 g/8 oz plain flour
40 g/1½ oz mixed peel
175 g/6 oz each of
currants, raisins
and sultanas
grated rind and juice
of 1 lemon
1 level tsp baking
powder
2 tbsp whisky
25 g/1 oz blanched
almonds
2 tbsp boiled milk
1 tbsp sugar

1

3

1. Cream the butter and sugar in a bowl. When they are light and fluffy, slowly add the four eggs, one at a time, plus a spoonful of flour with each, beating well all the time.

2. Stir in the dried fruits and the lemon rind and juice. Add the rest of the flour, sifted with the baking powder, and the whisky. Make sure the mixture is stirred well. If it is too stiff, add a little milk.

3. Place the mixture in a 20 cm/8 inch greased and lined cake tin and flatten the top with a spoon.

4. Cover with foil or greaseproof paper and bake at 170°C/325°C/ Gas Mark 3 for 2 hours. Halfway through the cooking time, take off the foil and arrange the split almonds in concentric circles on the top of the cake.

5. Check the cake with a skewer towards the end of cooking. If it is still uncooked in the middle, put it back for the full 2 hours.

6. About 5–10 minutes before the end of the cooking time, mix the boiled milk with the sugar. Brush the top with the sweetened milk to create a dry glaze.

7. Keep in the tin for 15 minutes before turning out on a wire tray and store in an airtight container when cool.

Fruity Apple Tea Bread

Ingredients

Cuts into 12 slices

125 g/4 oz butter
125 g/4 oz soft light brown sugar
275 g/10 oz sultanas
150 ml/¼ pint apple juice
1 eating apple, peeled cored and chopped
2 medium eggs, beaten
275 g/10 oz plain flour
½ tsp ground cinnamon
½ tsp ground ginger
2 tsp bicarbonate of soda
curls of butter, to serve

To decorate:

1 eating apple, cored and sliced
1 tsp lemon juice
1 tbsp golden syrup, warmed

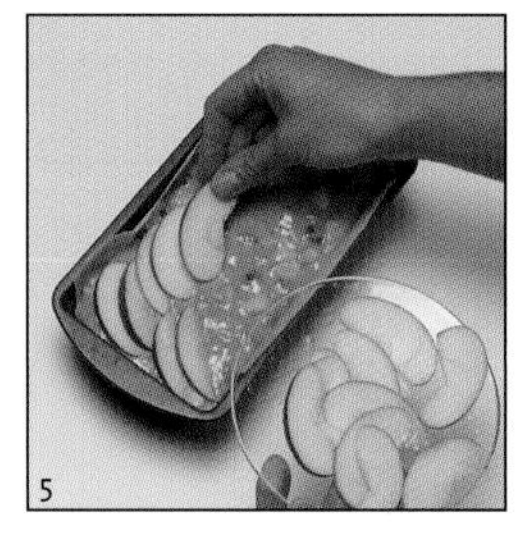

5

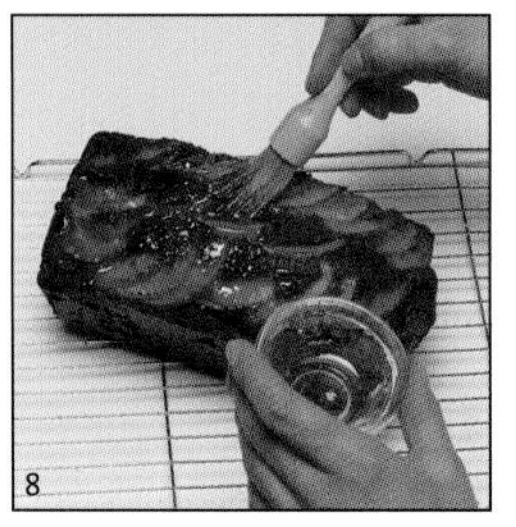

8

1 Preheat the oven to 180°C/350°F/Gas Mark 4. Oil and line the base of a 900 g/2 lb loaf tin with non-stick baking paper.

2 Put the butter, sugar, sultanas and apple juice in a small saucepan. Heat gently, stirring occasionally until the butter has melted. Tip into a bowl and leave to cool.

3 Stir in the chopped apple and beaten eggs. Sift the flour, spices and bicarbonate of soda over the apple mixture.

4 Stir into the sultana mixture, spoon into the prepared loaf tin and smooth the top level with the back of a spoon.

5 Toss the apple slices in lemon juice and arrange on top.

6 Bake in the preheated oven for 50 minutes or until a skewer inserted into the centre comes out clean. Cover with tinfoil to prevent the top from browning too much.

7 Leave in the tin for 10 minutes before turning out to cool on to a wire rack.

8 Brush the top with golden syrup and leave to cool. Remove the lining paper, then cut the cake into thick slices and serve with curls of butter.

Gingerbread

Ingredients
Cuts into 8 slices

175 g/6 oz butter
or margarine
225 g/8 oz black treacle
50 g/2 oz dark
muscovado sugar
350 g/12 oz plain flour
2 tsp ground ginger
150 ml/¼ pint
milk, warmed
2 medium eggs
1 tsp bicarbonate of soda
1 piece of stem ginger
in syrup
1 tbsp stem ginger syrup

2

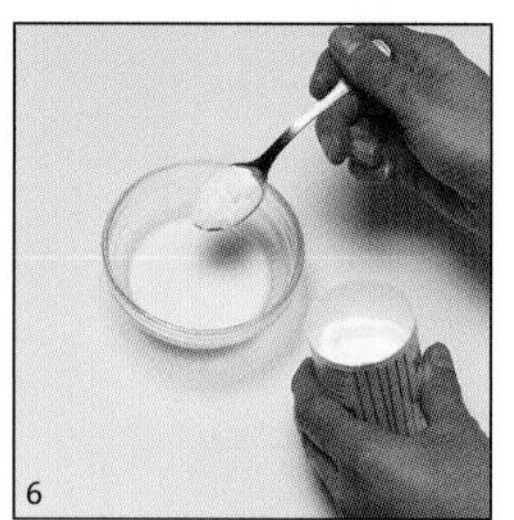
6

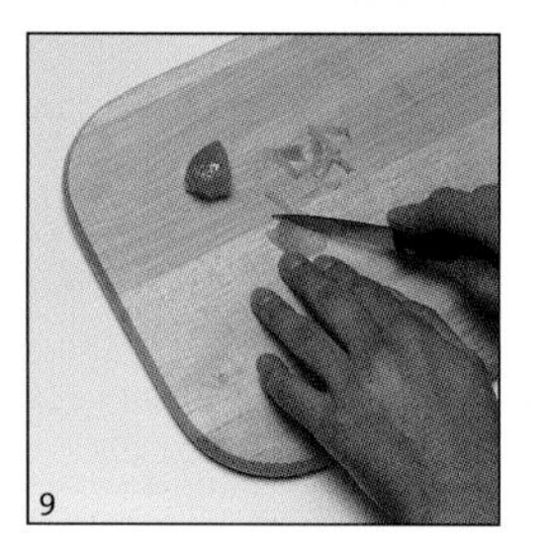
9

1 Preheat the oven to 150°C/300°C/Gas Mark 2, 10 minutes before baking. Lightly oil and line the base of a 20.5 cm/8 inch deep round cake tin with greaseproof or baking paper.

2 In a saucepan, gently heat the butter or margarine, black treacle and sugar, stirring occasionally until the butter melts. Leave to cool slightly.

3 Sift the flour and ground ginger into a large bowl.

4 Make a well in the centre, then pour in the treacle mixture. Reserve 1 tablespoon of the milk, then pour the rest of the milk into the treacle mixture. Stir together lightly until mixed.

5 Beat the eggs together, then stir into the mixture.

6 Dissolve the bicarbonate of soda in the remaining 1 tablespoon of warmed milk and add to the mixture.

7 Beat the mixture until well mixed and free of lumps.

8 Pour into the prepared tin and bake in the preheated oven for 1 hour, or until well risen and a skewer inserted into the centre comes out clean.

9 Cool in the tin, then remove. Slice the stem ginger into thin slivers and sprinkle over the cake. Drizzle with the syrup and serve.

Cloutie Dumpling

Ingredients
Serves 6

225 g/8 oz plain flour
100 g/4 oz shredded suet or margarine (margarine makes a lighter dumpling)
100 g/4 oz oatmeal
75 g/3 oz sugar
1 rounded tsp baking powder
225 g/8 oz mixed currants, sultanas and raisins
1–1½ tsp each ground cinnamon and mixed spice
1 tsp golden syrup
2 eggs, beaten
3–4 tbsp buttermilk

1 Sift the flour and rub in the suet or margarine in a large mixing bowl. Add all the other dry ingredients, including the fruit, and mix with a wooden spoon.

2 Make a well in the centre and add the syrup and eggs and mix well. Add enough buttermilk to make a soft but firm batter.

3 Lightly grease a pudding basin with melted butter and pour the pudding in. Allow a 2 cm/1 inch space at the top, even if this means throwing away some of the mixture – you will need the space for expansion.

4 Cover the basin with a greased sheet of foil and pour boiling water into a saucepan until it comes two-thirds of the way up the side. Boil for 3 hours.

5 Turn out the dumpling and serve either hot with custard or cold with cream.

CHEF'S TIP
The traditional way to cook a cloutie dumpling is in a muslin cloth or 'clout', hence the name. A tea towel can also be used. Dip in boiling water and flour well before adding the mixture. Tie the top, leaving room for expansion, then place on a plate in a saucepan. Cover with boiling water and cook for 2½–3 hours.

1

2

3

Black Bun

Ingredients
Serves 6–8

For the pastry case:
75 g/3 oz lard
75 g/3 oz butter
350 g/12 oz plain flour
pinch of salt

For the filling:
450 g/1 lb raisins
450 g/1 lb currants
50 g/2 oz blanched almonds, chopped
50 g/2 oz mixed peel, chopped
75 g/3 oz soft brown sugar
175 g/6 oz plain flour
1 level tsp ground allspice
½ level tsp each ground ginger, ground cinnamon, baking powder
1 generous pinch black pepper
½ tsp baking powder
1 tbsp brandy
1 large egg, beaten
milk to moisten

CHEF'S TIP
Black Bun is traditionally served at the end of the year at Hogmanay. Ideally it should be made several weeks in advance so that it can mature. It will keep for up to six months in an airtight container.

1. Grease an 20 cm/8 inch loaf tin. Rub the fats into the flour and salt and then mix in enough cold water to make a stiff dough – this will be lining the tin.

2. Roll out the pastry and cut into six pieces, using the bottom, top and four sides of the tin as a rough guide. Press the bottom and four side pieces into the tin, pressing the overlaps to seal the pastry shell.

3. Mix the raisins, currants, almonds, mixed peel and sugar together. Sift in the flour, all the spices and the baking powder and bind them together using the brandy and almost all the egg. Add enough milk to keep the mixture moist.

4. Pack the filling into the lined tin and add the pastry lid, pinching the edges and using milk or egg to seal really well. Lightly prick the surface with a fork and make four holes to the bottom of the tin with a skewer. Make a small depression in the centre, as it will rise as it cooks. Brush the top with milk or the rest of the egg to create a glaze.

5. Bake in a pre-heated oven at 160°C/325°F/Gas Mark 3 for 2½ to 3 hours. Test with a skewer – if it does not come out clean, continue cooking. Cool in the tin and then turn onto a wire rack.

1

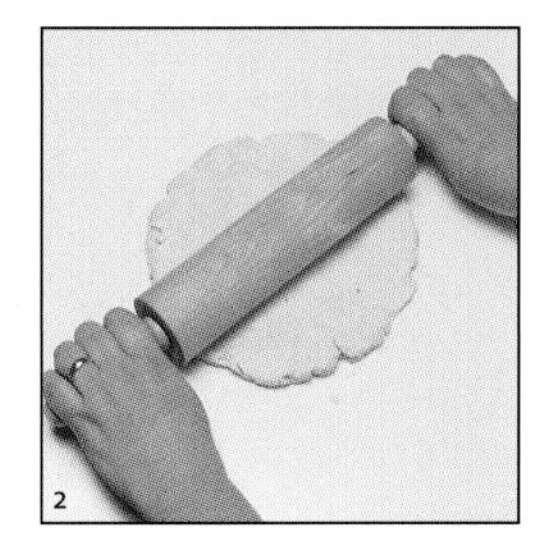
2

Traditional Oven Scones

Ingredients
Makes 8

225 g/8 oz
self-raising flour
1 tsp baking powder
pinch of salt
40 g/11/2 oz
butter, cubed
15 g/½ oz caster sugar
150 ml/¼ pint milk, plus
1 tbsp for brushing
1 tbsp plain flour,
to dust

Lemon & sultana scone variation:
50 g/2 oz sultanas
finely grated rind
of ½ lemon
beaten egg, to glaze

CHEF'S TIP
Nothing beats scones still warm from the oven. Split the scones open and fill with a layer of juicy strawberry jam and clotted cream. Serve the scones with a pot of tea for a delicious afternoon treat.

1 Preheat the oven to 220°C/425°F/Gas Mark 7, 15 minutes before baking. Sift the flour, baking powder and salt into a large bowl. Rub in the butter until the mixture resembles fine breadcrumbs. Stir in the sugar and mix in enough milk to give a fairly soft dough.

2 Knead the dough on a lightly floured surface for a few seconds until smooth. Roll out until 2 cm/¾ inch thick and stamp out 6.5 cm/2½ inch rounds with a floured plain cutter.

3 Place on an oiled baking sheet and brush the tops with milk. Do not brush it over the sides or the scones will not rise properly. Dust with a little plain flour.

4 Bake in the preheated oven for 12–15 minutes, or until well risen and golden brown. Transfer to a wire rack and serve warm or leave to cool completely. The scones are best eaten on the day of baking but may be kept in an airtight tin for up to two days.

5 For lemon and sultana scones, stir in the sultanas and lemon rind with the sugar. Roll out until 2 cm/¾ inches thick and cut into 8 fingers, 10 x 2.5 cm/4 x 1 inch in size. Bake the scones as before.

1

2

3

Oatmeal Raisin Biscuits

Ingredients
Makes 24

175 g/6 oz plain flour
150 g/5 oz rolled oats
1 tsp ground ginger
½ tsp baking powder
½ tsp bicarbonate of soda
125 g/4 oz soft light brown sugar
50 g/2 oz raisins
1 medium egg, lightly beaten
150 ml/¼ pint vegetable or sunflower oil
4 tbsp milk

1 Preheat the oven to 200°C/400°F/Gas Mark 6, 15 minutes before baking. Lightly oil a baking sheet.

2 Mix together the flour, oats, ground ginger, baking powder, bicarbonate of soda, sugar and the raisins in a large bowl.

3 In another bowl, mix the egg, oil and milk together. Make a well in the centre of the dry ingredients and pour in the egg mixture.

4 Mix the mixture together well with either a fork or a wooden spoon to make a soft but not sticky dough.

5 Place spoonfuls of the dough well apart on the oiled baking sheet and flatten the tops down slightly with the tines of a fork.

6 Transfer the biscuits to the preheated oven and bake for 10–12 minutes until golden.

7 Remove from the oven, leave to cool for 2–3 minutes, then transfer the biscuits to a wire rack to cool. Serve when cold or store in an airtight tin.

CHEF'S TIP
This dough can be made, wrapped in clingfilm then stored in the refrigerator for up to 1 week before baking. When ready to bake, simply cut off the dough and bake as above.

2

3

5

Dornoch Dreams

Ingredients
Makes 12

50 g/2 oz butter
or margarine
175 ml/6 fl oz water
100 g/4 oz plain flour
3 eggs
350 g/12 oz raspberries
(whole or lightly
crushed)
100 g/4 oz clear honey
300 ml/½ pint
double cream
2 tbsp Drambuie
icing sugar,
for decoration

1 Place the butter or margarine and water in a saucepan and heat until the fat has melted. Remove from the heat and stir in the flour.

2 Beat until the mixture forms a ball and leaves the edges of the pan cleanly. Beat the eggs and slowly add them, a little at a time, beating well between each addition until the mixture is smooth, shiny and of a piping consistency.

3 Spoon the pastry mixture into a large piping bag with a plain nozzle and pipe 12 round cakes onto a lightly greased baking tray.

4 Bake in the centre of a preheated oven at 200°C/400°F/Gas Mark 6 for 20–30 minutes until golden brown. Remove from the oven, pierce to allow the steam to escape and then leave to cool.

5 Mix the raspberries and honey. Stir the Drambuie into the whipped cream, then split the buns and fill with the raspberries and cream. Dust with the icing sugar and serve immediately.

1

2

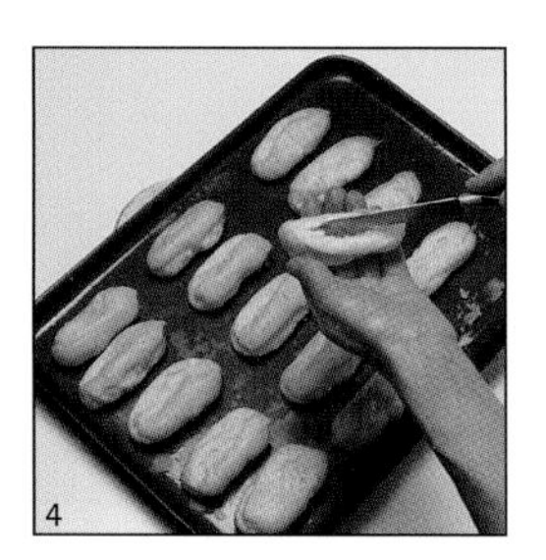
4

Butterscotch

Ingredients

Makes about 450 g/1 lb

150 ml/¼ pint water
1 tsp lemon juice
450 g/1 lb granulated sugar
¼ tsp cream of tartar
75 g/3 oz unsalted butter
¼ tsp vanilla essence

1. Oil a 28 x 18 cm/11 x 7 inch shallow baking tin well.

2. Put the water and lemon juice in a heavy-based saucepan and heat until slightly warm. Stir in the sugar and continue to heat gently, stirring with a wooden spoon until all the sugar has thoroughly dissolved. Do not allow it to boil.

3. Stir in the cream of tartar and bring to the boil until the mixture reaches 115°C/242°F on a sugar thermometer or until a teaspoonful of the mixture forms a soft ball when it is dropped into a cup of cold water.

4. Remove from the heat and beat in the butter. Return to the heat and boil to 138°C/280°F or until a teaspoonful of the mixture forms a thin thread when dropped into a cup of cold water. The thread will bend and break when pressed between your fingers.

5. Remove from the heat and beat in the vanilla essence. Pour into the oiled tin and leave until it is almost set before marking into small rectangles with a knife.

6. When it is completely set, break into pieces and store in an airtight container.

2

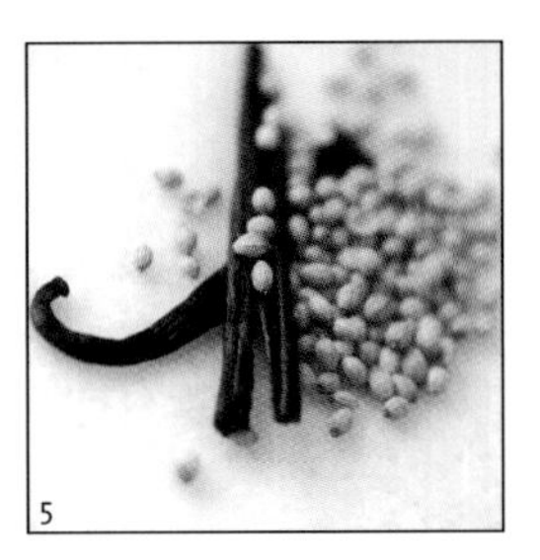

5

Shortbread Biscuits

Ingredients
Makes 36

225 g/8 oz
butter, softened
75 g/3 oz icing sugar
175 g/6 oz plain flour
hundreds and
thousands
sugar strands
chocolate drops
silver balls
50 g/2 oz icing sugar
2–3 tsp lemon juice

1 Preheat the oven to 180°C/350°F/Gas Mark 4, 10 minutes before baking. Lightly oil a baking sheet.

2 Cream the butter and icing sugar until fluffy. Gradually add the flour and continue beating for a further 2–3 minutes until it is smooth and light.

3 Roll into balls and place on a baking sheet. Cover half of the dough mixture with hundreds and thousands, sugar strands, chocolate drops or silver balls. Keep the other half plain.

4 Bake in the preheated oven for 6–8 minutes, until the bottoms are lightly browned. Remove from the oven and transfer to a wire rack to cool.

5 Sift the icing sugar into a small bowl. Add the lemon juice and blend until a smooth icing forms.

6 Using a small spoon, swirl the icing over the cooled plain biscuits. Decorate with either the extra hundreds and thousands, chocolate drops or silver balls and serve.

CHEF'S TIP

For a more sophisticated-looking biscuit, pipe the biscuits onto a baking sheet using a piping bag fitted with a large star nozzle.

2

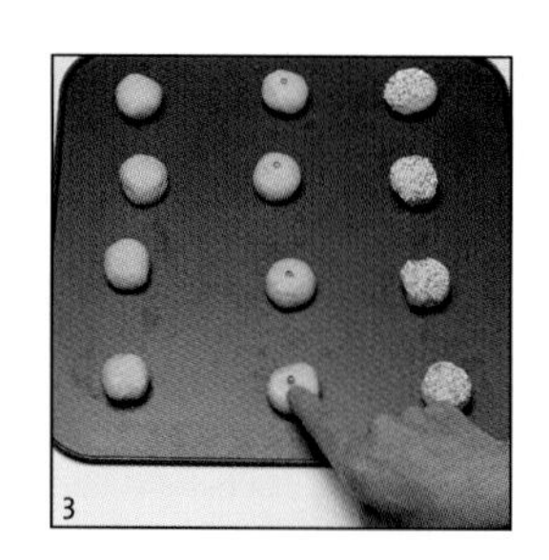
3

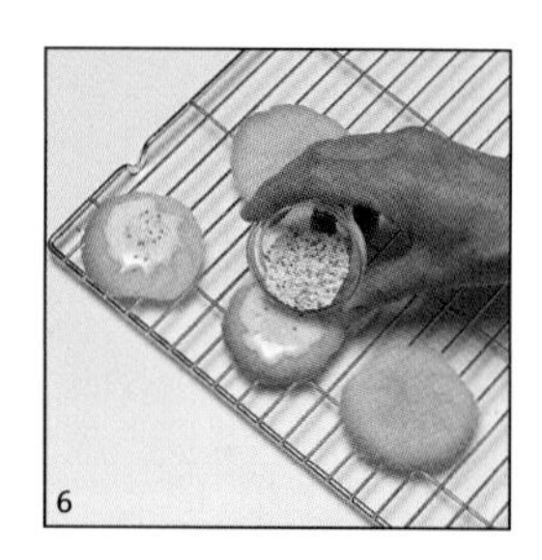
6

Caramel Shortbread

Ingredients
Makes 20

125 g/4 oz butter, softened
2 tbsp smooth peanut butter
75 g/3 oz caster sugar
75 g/3 oz cornflour
175 g/6 oz plain flour

For the topping:

200 g/7 oz caster sugar
125 g/4 oz butter
2 tbsp golden syrup
75 g/3 oz liquid glucose
75 ml/3 fl oz water
400 g can sweetened condensed milk
175 g/6 oz pecans, roughly chopped
75 g/3 oz plain dark chocolate
1 tbsp butter

2

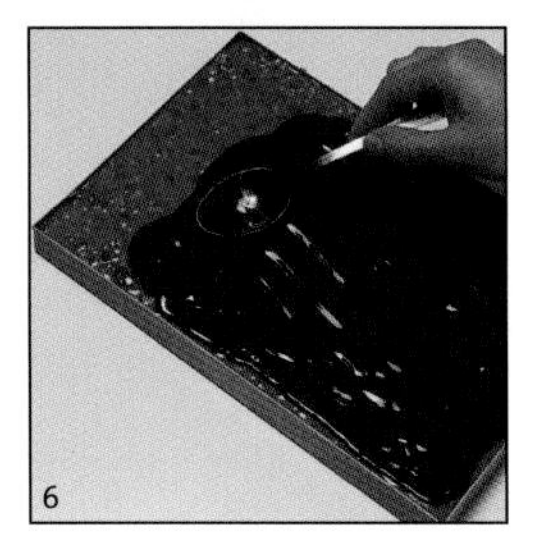
6

1 Preheat the oven to 180°C/350°F/Gas Mark 4, 10 minutes before baking. Lightly oil and line an 18 cm x 28 cm/7 x 11 inch tin with greaseproof or baking paper.

2 Cream together the butter, peanut butter and sugar until light. Sift in the cornflour and flour together and mix in to make a smooth dough. Press the mixture into the prepared tin and prick all over with a fork. Bake in the preheated oven for 20 minutes, until just golden. Remove from the oven.

3 To make the topping, combine the sugar, butter, golden syrup, glucose, water and milk in a heavy-based saucepan. Stir constantly over a low heat without boiling until the sugar has dissolved. Increase the heat and boil steadily, stirring constantly for about 10 minutes until the mixture turns a golden caramel colour.

4 Remove the saucepan from the heat and add the pecans. Pour over the shortbread base immediately. Allow to cool, then refrigerate for at least 1 hour.

5 Break the chocolate into small pieces and put into a heatproof bowl with the butter. Place over a saucepan of barely simmering water, ensuring that the bowl does not come into contact with the water. Leave until melted, then stir together well.

6 Remove the shortbread from the refrigerator and pour the chocolate evenly over the top, spreading thinly to cover. Leave to set, cut into squares and serve.

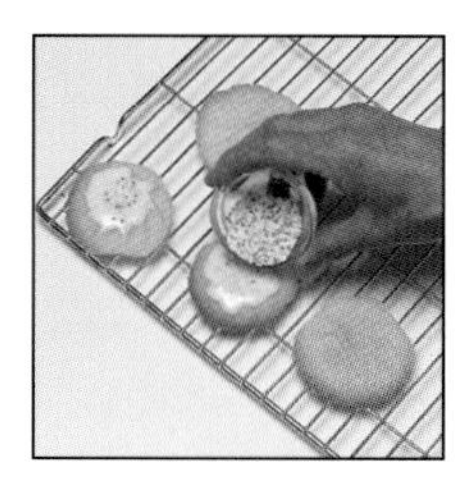

LOMOND

Lomond Books Ltd
Broxburn, EH52 5NF, Scotland
www.lomondbooks.com

NOTE

Recipes using uncooked eggs should be avoided by infants, the elderly, pregnant women and anyone suffering from an illness.

14 16 18 17 15 13

5 7 9 10 8 6 4

ISBN: 978-1-84204-078-2

The CIP record for this book is available from the British Library

Printed in Singapore

ACKNOWLEDGEMENTS

Authors: Catherine Atkinson, Juliet Barker, Liz Martin, Gina Steer, Carol Tennant, Mari Mereid Williams, Elizabeth Wolf-Cohen, Simone Wright

With thanks to www.rampantscotland.com

Project Editor: Sarah Goulding
Designer: Lucy Robins
Production: Chris Herbert

Photography: Colin Bowling and Paul Forrester
Home Economists and Stylists: Jacqueline Bellefontaine, Mandy Phipps, Vicki Smallwood and Penny Stephens
All props supplied by Barbara Stewart at Surfaces